Pillar Talk

(or Backcloth and Ashes)

A theatrical sketch for Saint Symeon Stylites and column

By **Edward Petherbridge**

Bearing only the most superficial resemblance to the historical 5th Century Syrian saint

authorHOUSE

1663 LIBERTY DRIVE, SUITE 200
BLOOMINGTON, INDIANA 47403
(800) 839-8640
WWW.AUTHORHOUSE.COM

© *2005 Edward Petherbridge. All Rights Reserved.*

No part of this book may be reproduced, stored in a retrieval system, or transmitted by any means without the written permission of the author.

First published by AuthorHouse 07/18/05

ISBN: 1-4208-6792-X (sc)

Printed in the United States of America
Bloomington, Indiana

This book is printed on acid-free paper.

For Neil Fitzpatrick

First performed by Edward Petherbridge
on the Edinburgh Festival Fringe
at the Pleasance JackDome on August 3rd 2005

ACKNOWLEDGMENTS

Does any body bother to read the acknowledgments?

Someone once told me that he had to start the day by reading, even if there was nothing to hand but a cereal packet, so it is possible that someone in such extremis may one day turn to this page with gratitude. I begin by mentioning, not by name, a publisher who, knowing that this play was a one act play for the Edinburgh Festival Fringe, turned it down because he thought it was "too short"; a sort of Polonius in reverse.

Heartfelt thanks for the support of my family, particularly our daughter Dora who has performed wonderfully as a PA and secretary and sat through various trial readings as a sensitively critical audience.

Friends contributed tremendous help and encouragement, attending a rehearsed reading of a first draft: they included many of my colleagues from the cast of *The Woman In White*. Many thanks to Caroline Blakiston who has been a fine champion and her sister Rachel who unknowingly was instrumental in my going to

Syria where I met wonderful people. Thanks to Roy and Hilary King of the Red Pear theatre for their enthusiastic and generous material support of the Fringe production.

ILLUSTRATIONS

The Bradford Tram photographs are from the J. W. Pitts Collection by kind permission of Councillor Stanley King with the cooperation of the West Yorkshire Archive, Bradford.

All other photographs were taken by Edward Petherbridge and the charcoal drawing of him is a self portrait. The fifth century Syrian carving of John the Baptist baptising Jesus and the sixth century pilgrim's token are in the British Museum, Petherbridge's photographs of them are © Copyright The Trustees of The British Museum.

PREFACE

And as he journeyed, he came near Damascus: and suddenly there shined round about him a light from heaven:

Acts of the Apostles Ch. 9 v3.

I've been surprised, not to say appalled, by the number of young people of my acquaintance, some of them at least nominally confirmed into the Church of England, for whom the words *"The road to Damascus"* ring absolutely no bells. What *do* they teach them in RE? This morning, I wanted to find the New Testament passage describing the pivotal incident in Saul/Paul's life which has resonated throughout Christendom for almost two thousand years, and until recently could be referred to to with confidence at dinner parties and barbeques to describe a conversion to anything from Blue Eyed Soul to faith in the Euro. (All is not entirely lost; I was astonished to hear from my daughter that a friend of her's who at Leeds University is in her third year at the college of Art, not a temple of any kind of tradition these days one would have thought - astonished to hear that the girl and several fellow students, including some from the drama and dance departments, have joined a Christian fundamentalist sect (at any rate they don't hold with Darwin's theories) called New Frontiers. Clearly the road to Damascus has a branch near Woodhouse Lane.

First thing this morning I picked up a little Khaki bound Bible with its inscription in purple ink;

Rehoboth Sunday School
Presented to Willie Petherbridge
on the occasion of him joining His Majesties Forces during
The Great European War
1914 To.

My father must have wondered, at the age of sixteen, where the *"To"* was leading and how long it would take.

The Bible more or less fell open at the right page. It was the sort of happening that Rehoboth Methodist Chapel ministers and some Sunday school teachers often gave as evidence in hushed tones of the work of "a hidden hand", a hand clearly less adept at intervening in such slaughterous occurrences as The Great

xii ⇒ Edward Petherbridge

European War. My father never talked about his war experience or anything else much, for that matter. All I know is that some of it was in Egypt and he dealt with cavalry horses. Once, on the sands at Bridlington when I was a boy, I was amazed to see him talking to the donkey ride man who also had a horse or it might have been a large pony - what did I know? Soon my father was charging down the beach on this steed, and then saying, as if nothing had happened," It had no *Go* in it"

Clearly there was more to my dad than the silent, tea total, allotment tending wool warehouseman I knew, but I wouldn't be at all surprised if my dad never opened that little khaki bible. His eyesight was never good and its print is extremely small, and I never had any glimpses of a fervent faith. The Bradford Methodists I was brought up amongst, with a few exceptions, were working and lower middle class versions of J.B. Priestley's characters in *When We Are Married*. Chapel going was to do with respectability. The goings on in the Holy Land of Holy Writ were at once familiar and utterly distant and foreign.

There wasn't a lot of truck with saints; certainly not saints' *days,* which they'd have called Jiggery Popery if their taciturn disapproval of statues, Latin and incense, robes and genuflections had been expressed in word play. My road, or rather BA Flight to Damascus a week or so ago, was immediately preceded by a flying visit to my home town, where, at Rehoboth Methodist Sunday School and my C of E Elementary, I'd developed the sun drenched imaginative pictures of the landscape and happenings in the Gospel that are still programmed into my grey matter, along with the light from heaven as Saul of Tarsus heard, *Saul, Saul, why persecuteth thou me?*

In the West Yorkshire Archive, I found a different kind of picture, a 1945 photograph of the vanished townscape of my youth: the number 11 tram toiling up Bowling Old Lane past the forbidding bulk of the long demolished Rehoboth, its notice board bearing a poster for the Harvest Festival in which, just turned nine years old, I almost certainly sang a solo. It was amongst the dark satanic mill chimneys in this picture that the small congregation would sing:

Summer suns are glowing over land and sea
Happy light is flowing, bountiful and free
All the earth rejoices in the mellow rays
All earth's thousand voices
Swell the psalm of praise

-as the evening sun filtered through the sooty "frosted" glass windows.

We had neighbours in the next street who were very odd I thought; a slight, pale middle aged married couple. I'd see them singing hymns on Saturday afternoons down in the town by Oastler's Monument in Rawson Square. When I was twenty I met the lady of this couple in the street near our house when I was paying a visit home. I'd come through a little saga of conscientious objection and been released from a spell in Wormwood Scrubs. It was the first time I'd ever spoken to her and she turned out to be, not only perfectly "normal" and sweet, but the only person in remarkably tolerant West Bowling to be completely unembarrassed and neither puzzled nor offended about what I'd done. She talked of how she and her late husband had been ostracised during the Second War because they'd belonged to the Peace Pledge Union.

Talking of extreme positions, and leaving aside, for example, President George Bush's recent intervention to try to preserve the life of the lady contraversially hospitalised on long term life support, whilst countenancing

Pillar Talk = xv

"collateral damage" elsewhere, there's no doubt about it; if Symeon Stylites were alive in Britain today, he would be sectioned under the mental health act, or he'd be standing in Oxford Circus by the entrance to the tube at rush hour, haranguing uncaring, embarrassed commuters through a loud hailer, making "Christ died for your sins" sound like a shouted head line from The Evening Standard. I remember a man from the nineteen seventies who was often to be seen there, wearing a sandwich board and carrying a placard; he was covered in lists of forbidden protein foods, all of which, we were warned, induced passion. (I have eaten beans and lentils in hopes ever since.)

However one bends over backwards to give Symeon the benefit of our modern doubts, or even forwards, genuflecting as Symeon could on top of his pillar, his head touching his toes we're told because his fasting stomach was so small, - actually he was a serial genuflector, and could get up to a thousand and more in one session(!) – however one bends, one cannot see him as the living icon his contemporaries so revered. He would not let a woman into his sight, not even his mother. One sees the rejection of the things of "this world" by the leaders of the ascetic movement as an aberration. It is not

xvi ⚊ Edward Petherbridge

only that so many of us have ceased to believe in heaven and that self fulfilment in *this* world is the order of our day, it is that we have loved and lusted for, and exploited the things of this world to such a degree: we know we have damaged it, perhaps beyond recall and that makes us worship its fragile wonders and splendours all the more, increasing our concern for our own survival in this precious life upon it.

Mind you, I can report, being a latter day pilgrim to the remains of Symeon's pillar, that he picked a beautiful plot of this earth for himself, an elevated location commanding a view that I can imagine myself contemplating for thirty six years without complaint. It's the kind of view that is enough to make Richard Dawkins believe in God - no, perhaps not: I've just looked up *God* in the index of his *River Out of Eden* to be confronted by,

"*See* Religion; Utility function"

His chapter, *'God's Utility Function'*, ends, famously, by quoting…

"that unhappy poet Houseman"

For Nature, heartless witless Nature
Will neither know nor care.

Pillar Talk ⚍ xvii

And Dawkins adds:

DNA neither knows nor cares. DNA just is. And we dance to its music.

Symeon could spot his pilgrims miles off, as they could spot him. He concerned himself with this world to the degree of mediating on local land and cattle ownership, according to at least one reference book, and the Emperor Leo I was influenced by him according to another. One smells a rat as soon as one reads that after his death, powdered stone from his pillar was available to be taken internally as a cure in exchange for suitable gifts to the impressive pilgrims' basilica built on the site.

One day I will seek out Symeon's extant sermons and hymns and prayers. I began writing *Pillar Talk* before I knew there were any, and before I knew that it was comparatively simple and not at all perilous to make the journey to Syria to see what remains of his pillar, in fact before I knew there still really was a pillar.

I'd been writing something else, about my boyhood, thinking about the plays I saw and acted in at school, and decided to revisit some of them in the reading room of The British Theatre Museum. Did I harbour a hope that a play called

Symeon Stylites, which I remembered another group of boys acting, might have a leading part for me in my old age? We had a prefect at Grange Grammar School in Bradford who I can see across more than half a century, sitting cross legged on top of a rostrum and saying, "I will sit here for an immense period". He was a tall, unkempt, bony faced young man, who ranged about the school, a rather anarchic member of the brainy set who made up the tiny sixth form. He'd pull a water pistol out from under his jacket and, with an unsmiling casual devil-may-care expression, spray whole lines of us younger boys as we stood waiting to go into our classes. I both deplored and admired the way, as a prefect, he chose to stand inside and outside the law. Water pistols were contraband on pain, and I mean pain, of severe punishment.

The pillar was the star of the school production, though scenically it was crude, rudimentary. It was the *idea* of it. There was something intrinsically suspenseful and fascinating about the situation of the hero that lingered in my imagination though I'd forgotten all the detail, not even remembering that Symeon's last visitor was The Devil. I do remember my great friend in the A stream, (I was always in the C stream) - looking disturbingly ravishing as the Lady Pilgrim, though there was "never any thing between us", as plays on Saturday night Theatre on the BBC Home Service radio used to put it, rather oddly now I come to think of it - nothing more than a passion for theatricals. It was he who opened up a road for me simply by saying, "There's a Sunday newspaper, two actually, which give an entire page to the theatre and the cinema and the arts, and you can read whole articles every week on the latest West End plays." Probably the most important discovery of my fourteenth year was finding the enjoyment of comparing the views of the two critical Titans, Kenneth Tynan and Harold Hobson, and dreaming of seeing for myself what they so tantalisingly described.

Rediscovering the play about St. Symeon by one F. Fladen Smith was a disappointment. I may as well say that I thought I could do better. There was still that fascination with the impossible premise.

My effort was never going to be religious drama as I'd understood it when I was a theatre school student, (nor is Fladen Smith's) studying the history of drama from the Greeks, through the Mystery and Miracle plays, Everyman, right up to T.S. Eliot.

Now I find it impossible to believe in divine intervention and am puzzled and alienated by the whole concept of sacrifice and propitiation. (The oldest Christian altars I saw in Syria, thought to be early fourth century, had a raised lip all round their edges, like altars for animal sacrifice had had) Organised religion had little allure for me when I was a boy, and it didn't help that the Methodists had dispensed with altars. My parents were *dis*organised about it, I think on account of the severe stroke my mother had just before I was born, so I was never baptised, though I went to our local Methodist Sunday school. I did go to the lengths of getting baptised by an Actors' Church Union parson when I was twenty and in the rep. at Scarborough. He conducted the ceremony in a little modern church on a council estate on the characterless outskirts and kept on referring to, "this congregation here present", though there were only the two of us. Then he shocked me by inviting me into his vicarage for a whisky: as a Methodist, I'd signed the pledge of total abstinence at the age of twelve. I compromised and asked for a small sherry.

By contrast, my conformation into The C.of E. was startlingly grand. I was part of a sizable job lot in the soaring surroundings of

York Minster, but I only remember feeling detached and tainted that day amongst the little girls in white dresses, and was sure none of it had properly "taken", despite the fact that by then I had suffered the mild privations of being imprisoned, just turned twenty, for three months for mistiming my Christian conscientious objection to National Service, that's to say, objecting during it rather than before.

In Syria, a few days ago, I stood in the great mosque in Damascus and touched the shrine containing John the Baptist's head. I went, as St. Paul had been commanded to go, to the street that is called Straight. In a Christian church outside Damascus I heard The Lord's Prayer spoken in Aramaic, the language of Jesus, and was jostled afterwards by pilgrims anxious to buy mass produced religious pictures in the crowded souvenir shop adjacent to the church with its early fourth century altars. Experientially, the "real thing" remained illusive until I got to the ruins of the basilica of Symeon Stylites where several things happened.

In *Pillar Talk,* there is the totally invented, small but important off stage character of a dog. (I sound like an agent trying to sell a part to a pup.)There were four dogs in the ruins that afternoon, and of course I believed they were descendents of my dog; very friendly they were and quite on their own. Nobody I talked to had seen them there before. Near the plinth on which the peculiar egg shaped remnant of the pillar sits was a Muslim family. The mother, dressed in black with her hair veiled, was sitting on a huge fallen stone, breast feeding her baby. (How appalled, I suddenly bethink myself, Symeon would have been.) A little later I saw them again under some trees outside the shaded eastern wall, the interior of the ruin ablaze with the evening sun, the opposite hill greenish gold. Some children, appearing no bigger than tiny coloured beetles played amongst the trees, lumps of limestone and farm animals, their voices blending with the musical chiming of sheep bells. We turned and looked at one another; "Beautiful" the father of the family said in English, "I am Syrian, my wife is from Bulgaria. I am a doctor."

"I am English. I am an actor" I replied. The declaration of one's Englishness in Syria was, in my experience, always greeted by a happy smile, sometimes clouded with a frown for Tony Blair. I think my status as actor might have been the cue for him to offer me a Syrian cigarette which I accepted. A plastic cup of Syrian cola was poured for me.

"Cigarette called *Alhambra*" he said.

"Last week", I told him, "I was in my home town in England photographing the first theatre I ever went to; it's called The Alhambra."

In our search for significance, we treat coincidences as signs.

"That is my brother" the doctor continued, "His name Abdullah." We shook hands and I told them that when I was a boy, actors in plays always smoked and every theatre programme carried the words "Cigarettes by Abdullah" (I made no remarks about stockings by Kayser Bondor and wardrobe care by Lux). Then the mother handed the baby to her daughter who gave it to me to hold; a plump baby girl, satisfied and drowsy with milk but, sensing a change in ambiance, she opened her eyes a little and regarded me placidly as part of the benign universe to which she was accustomed.

We parted, conscious that in some way we were affirming the brotherhood of man. Soon I was alone and back contemplating what was left of Symeon's stone. I thought of my old friend since the sixties, Neil Fitzpatrick, to whom my play is dedicated. He's been a life long Catholic. I asked him about his faith for the fist time a month or so ago when I phoned him in Australia to find that his cancer had recurred and he was about to undergo further chemotherapy. I asked him what he felt about the existence of an afterlife, "That's none of my business" he said, "and certainly I don't hold with being 'good' now, in the hope of reward later. I go to the lowest available mass, (the theatre does processions and dressing up and ritual so much better) - and there are bits of the creed I remain silent throughout, but", he said, "the nub is simply what Christ said - love your neighbour and, (the hard bit) - love your enemies."

I noticed a little weed growing out of the crevice between the plinth and the boulder shaped remains of the pillar. I plucked it and pressed it into my note book and then saw a soft looking part of the stone that seemed to have signs as having been scratched at. It turned out not to be soft at all, but I managed to get a grain or two of the stone under the nail of my right index finger, then I drew my finger up to my lips and murmured a prayer for my friend, irrespective of whether our DNA knows or cares.

Back in Damascus, whilst I thought about the price I was being asked to pay for a bell I was thinking I might use as a prop in the play, the owner of the shop in the souk near Straight Street offered to put me on the way to the famous spot, and we 'happened' to meet a young man who, the shop owner said, for no charge, would be my guide and then bring me back to the shop. Within moments the young man was not only showing me the great Mosque nearby, and the subterranean Christian church in Straight Street, and various nooks and crannies, but telling me his philosophy of life. Something like- "I have Muslim Friends and Christian friends and we get on very well. I was brought up Muslim and I believe in living a clean life and being straight and honest and not taking advantage or harming any one or being deceitful, but I don't need a book or any priests to tell me. I know what is right and wrong; the religions are there to control the people and get money."

I bought him a beer and we sat in the shade of a grape vine and put the world and Blair and Bush to rights - "Democracy?" he said, "Do you feel safe here? Would you rather live in America in one of those cities where you are free not to walk out after dark for fear of being shot?"

Back in the souk, the shop owner suggested after all that I should give my guide ten pounds, saw how much I liked the bell and poured me a third small glass of very sweet tea whilst a boy was prematurely wrapping the bell in newspaper.

****

I described the first draft of *Pillar Talk*, or *Backcloth and Ashes* as "a Scherzo for saint and pillar", but it got longer and developed a little too much largo. The real Symeon's preoccupation with the mortification of the flesh doesn't interest me, nor does what we'd call his religiosity. What's left for the top of my pillar?

Climb it, if you will, and see.

Oh, about the pillar: the first thing people ask me is if I'm going to perform the play on one. Their disappointment when I've suggested that the pillar might be entirely imaginary has been palpable. At Tom Stoppard's bi-annual garden party the other day, Tom joked that I could have a foot or so of the height of the pillar showing, and the floor surrounding it covered by a cloud of dry ice! I've wondered what he might really do with the subject.

It so happens that I came across a quaint device the other day that might be elaborated upon and adapt to the stage beautifully, providing a bit of theatrical trickery, a diverting scenic prologue. It would get all but the imaginary pillar over and done with at the outset, leaving the stage clear for higher things.

London, 7th June 2005

Self Portrait, 2005.

Bowling Old Lane, Bradford 1945

xxx ⇌ Edward Petherbridge

Alhambra Theatre, Bradford c. 1945

**The Remnants of the Pillar and
Basilica at Deir Semaan, near Aleppo**

xxxii ⇒ Edward Petherbridge

Pillar Talk.

Or Backcloth and Ashes, a theatrical sketch for saint and pillar.

The auditorium lights dim. A small coup de teatre should take place to begin with, not so spectacular as to leave the audience hoping for more where it came from and idly bent on the play itself which, let's face it, is just a man talking. (At the time of writing the coup is still on the drawing board and defies description- in any case, description would destroy the coup factor) Before we see Simeon, in the dark we hear a sky lark and what could be a Syrian shepherd's pipe and the occasional cow bell. A voice with a Middle Eastern accent accompanies this evocative sound track:

"Some one thousand five hundred years ago, a hermit who had been a monk, and before that a shepherd, left his cave to live on top of an eight foot stone pillar. Eventually the pillar was increased in height to fifty feet and Simeon Stylites, the first pillar dweller, died up there after living thus for thirty six years".

The scene is the modest sized space on top of a high free standing stone pillar in Syria, one early morning in 469A.D. There is an elaborate marble chair in the Eastern Imperial style placed diagonally in one corner and a small weathered three legged stool is nearby, the only thing, it turns out, that Simeon Stylites ever sits on besides the floor. He is sixty nine years old, white haired, bearded, and discovered laying a sleep on the bare stone, dressed in the simplest possible monk's robe. There is, whether we can see it or not, a railing to prevent Simeon or anyone visiting (by way of a ladder) from falling off. A minimalist design: an off white square floor delineating the space on top of the pillar,- perhaps merging at the rear with the backcloth, which might appear to be made of sun bleached sack cloth serving as sky .It tells us little. Simeon will tell us more.

Simeon: (*Waking*) What a singularly dreadful dream. I pray my death will not be like that. Another dawn, I thank thee. Grant me curiosity to greet it as my first, and strength, tenderness and hope in case it is my last.

(*Pause*)

I must think of a better morning prayer. (*He paces round the top of his pillar as if in dictation mode- as in "take a letter miss*

Prendergast" – thereby defining the space for us) New Morning Prayer- that is to say, radically new morning prayer; *(mimetically he grasps the, to us until now, invisible railing round the edge of his platform and gazes down*) -prayer from the pillar of doubt. Lord- as usual my first thoughts on waking were of myself rather than my neighbour, or even my neighbours, who, mindful of the advantages, material and spiritual, of living in the benign shadow of my "holy" pillar, are- if not from Heaven – then careful at least, not to gain a reputation for being from the other place - thank God. I am, I hope, no cause for the sin of covetousness in my neighbour: conversely, I have never entertained hopes of having his ox nor his ass up here- still less his wife- though in earlier years it was touch and go in regard to his servant and his maid. It didn't occur to them to visit me, and I never risked my reputation by sending either of them an invitation saying "come up and see me some time" – but perhaps that was because I knew they couldn't read. A moral balance was achieved.

Here we are! Blessed - Roman roads, connecting Antioch with the Euphrates, a rich traffic of trade, silk from China, local harvests of olive oil and nuts, spices etc, -beautiful dawns and sunsets, remarkable building schemes I hear, producing majestic basilicas and monasteries noble in their austerity - where the conservative weep in their cells and seek thee in the blank walls thereof, as well as in the arc of sky above the cloister and each handful of the soil they till. The progressive study and translate Greek philosophy producing fine illuminated manuscripts, in the face of satirical rumours that they spend their time disputing how many angels can dance on a pin head. All this makes the region a very passable substitute for the Garden of Eden, and the populous amongst the olive groves and corn, are doing their best to sin as originally as possible…

but…

I have a difficult question for you this morning. I will not be in the least surprised if you leave me to answer it for myself; nor will I claim that the answer, if answer there is, is divinely inspired. My question… my quest… First I must ask, what guarantee have I that you had the time or inclination to listen to any of that…? It is my massive presumptuousness rather than thy omnipotent attention span I call into question-

(Something distracts his attention from God and he notices the audience)

- Good morning! I assume *you* did… listen to that (if not I am in trouble!) So there you are - cast as God's surrogate already without an audition! - Can't be bad. Usually I do not give audience until later in the day, but thirty six years on top of a pillar in 5th Century Syria, frees the spirit from dependence on routine. Spiritually speaking, I'm on a constant quest for the faintest variations in it. It is only Jesus Christ who can afford to be "the same yesterday, today and tomorrow"…. and you can imagine that the narrow limitations of a life of self denial up here give one a nose for faint variations, and transport one into extraordinary breadths of experience on several planes…

… though on the face of it my routine is simplicity itself; solitude, silence, prayer and contemplation in the mornings, perhaps some reading and correspondence too. I am determined not to let the papyrus work get me down. Letters arrive from the other side of the empire and beyond, I always reply - (mine could be the first pillar box.) I receive news of distant wars, floods, earthquakes, - requests for prayers in connection with the same- reports of weeping statues and the like, even good news worthy of credence occasionally; then in the afternoon during the pilgrim season, as much varied international human company as I can decently manage…

(*Deep breath*) - So:

I couldn't be more delighted to see you.

We meet - pilgrims and strangers in the world - "Be not forgetful to entertain strangers; for thereby some have entertained angels unawares"…

(*Simeon notices an elderly lady with shopping who has appeared in the aisle. He watches from his hermitical posture, waiting for the situation to resolve itself. The lady looks uncertainly at the stage and the audience, spots a seat and sits, arranging her shopping bags beside her discreetly; pause*)

Simeon: What a singularly dreadful dream. I pray my death will not be like that. Another Dawn, I thank thee… (The *lady gathers her shopping and leaves*)

Pause.

Lost souls in search of stand up comedy - (The Lord He gives and The Lord He taketh away) - are one thing: any pilgrim with a head for heights who approaches me in the **conventional** manner and makes it up the fifty feet of my ladder - is quite another- (I did the climb **once.** - You won't ever catch me on that ladder again) - The view from up here today…

6 ⇒ Edward Petherbridge

leaves a lot to the imagination.

Ever and never the same.

Thus far, *we* are only fragments of figments of one another's imagination. Some say we are each figments of our own imagination, but I rather think we are figments of God's imagination. Imagine! At any rate we are his children and imagination runs in the family.

It is, you may think, a massive imaginative pretence to live as I live.... We all live by pretence to a degree, but at this moment - *this* moment, now that the disparate trajectories of all or lives have lead us, undeniably - it would seem unavoidably, to this encounter- here on the fringe, on the edge of all manner of possibilities we could drop mere pretence and, please God, the pretentious, in favour of *let's pretend,* the game we all played habitually and so seriously once upon a time. These last days I've been observing a litter of sophisticated domesticated kittens playing it down there. The little girl at the farm asked my brethren if they would send her favourite up in my delivery basket for me to see. I have the little stigma to prove it. *(shows a long scratch on the inside of his forearm.)* I watched them feigning upon one another at the end of their games of chase, that fatal attack to the vulnerable base at the back of the neck;-rehearsing instinctively for the day when they'd hunt their prey to the kill in earnest.

A fox got them; every one.

Moral beings that we are- *our* childhood games of chase were called *Goodies and Baddies*, *Follow My Leader*, rehearsals too for our adult roles. There was *Mothers and Fathers*, which I only ever took to the let's pretend stage. Let's Pretend- trying on grown up reality for size and style in search of a true fit. But then our elders and betters taught us **pretence** so that we would cut our coats according to the prescribed cloth. Pretence – the most elaborate game of all.

Back to actuality and on with the show! - Not surprised, my **real life** pilgrim, as he peeps over on to the top of my pillar to find me wrapped - (*longish pause. Symeon perfectly still,-wrapped in fact - looking diagonally downwards, away from the direction of the top of the ladder, hands peacefully folded, at last he speaks in this attitude without moving*)- or unwrapped as the case may be - apparently oblivious of his - or occasionally her- presence. (*He becomes direct and informal again*) Call it my fourth wall syndrome. (*stands*) Please don't think that

8 ⇒ Edward Petherbridge

Christian Byzantium hasn't thought of *that* one. I, who have existed without walls for so long, know how to value the magical fourth. *(He steps forward and touches the invisible fourth wall, and scratches a small sign of the cross into its surface - then adopts, one after the other, three classic poses as he leans on it in "solitary" contemplation)*

(direct *again*) Wonderful thing,

(slapping his hand on it as on the flank of a horse, whilst contriving to synchronise the appropriate sound with the other against his buttock) - enabling *you* to see what you're most curious about-

(whispers) - what I'm really like when you're not there. *(Perhaps he peeps at the audience round the imaginary edge of the fourth wall then pushes himself off from it, turning his back to walk up stage, scratching his bum. Turns, mouths inaudibly, realises, reaches high to hook his fingers over the top of the wall, strenuously pulls himself up and climbs to stand on top.)* The secret theatre of solitude, the form most heavily dependent on your willing suspension of disbelief - *(jumps down)* - your disbelief, which some of you have already managed to suspend, against impossible odds, above the ritual of our meeting - a little uneasily - like

a pendulum in an earth tremor, or a sword of Damocles. (*turns to walk up stage, bumps into the wall, and, a little impatiently snaps his fingers to "vanish" it)*

Of course my **real life** pilgrim visitors, rich or poor, are predisposed to belief of some kind or another, or to the hope of it at least, having invested weeks, often months of travel.

My instinct with them is to achieve an early "*aha*" moment; *aha,* or even *ha ha* is an involuntary reaction and useful in the peculiar circumstances of a first meeting when there is an air of constraint, due to the pilgrim's attempt to *suppress* the involuntary, to be on his best behaviour, to veil surprise or disappointment, to fend off the need to fart, which the climb up my ladder seems to induce in the faithful. All first meetings are essentially improvisational of course - mine more so, there being no precedents for these vertiginous encounters after the white knuckled, breathless climb, and consequently no protective cloud of protocol. Some kneel, especially if it's windy, and cling to the railing. On a fine day they might move to kiss the hem of my garment, which I don't encourage. When to or three are gathered together, the stakes are high; it helps that we have One Lord, - even so we must extemporise and create more common, common ground, a dynamic, mutual plane of expectations and assumptions, however ramshackle, so that, as the phrase goes, we know where we are. This is where, eventually, the double meaning or the remark at once *apposite* and *inappropriate* comes in; another plane of assumptions and understanding collides, tips our situation on its axis and we share an educative glimpse of our absurdity - the *aha* moment. I trust I make myself clear. Perhaps I take the opportunity to theorise too much. Humour - that is to say the joke- is after all not pure, but **applied** science (and in this region, attracts commercial sponsorship from the water sellers.)

There is doubt of course. Whatever doubts they have that I might, after all, be a fake, they would be hard put to it to say what kind of fake exactly. They sometimes feel the same about God, or rather they suspect that God the Mystery is one thing, and the orthodox wisdom, "revelation" and paraphernalia surrounding Him, quite another; that or, more usually, it's the paraphernalia they adhere to. They can't wait to posses the pilgrims' token, made from the clay at the base of my pillar, so that they can say to God and their friends with modest fervour – *I have been there. I have done that*

- *there is the ladder I ascended.*

Paraphernalia; I'm sure you know unrepentant sinners with exquisite taste in sacred music and architecture. (I heard the other day of a cardinal who surprised some young priests at a seminar with, "All sin is tasteless: discuss.")

My paraphernalia, my pillar, is first glimpsed on the horizon and the dot on top of it is me; so that much is true. How many angels can dance on the top of Simeon's pillar?

Answer; it depends on the size of the orchestra; *(in response to the laugh)* - I thank you, *(beatifically)* at times I am entirely supported by involuntary contributions.

The point is I am there, as promised, as the reports and souvenirs and word of mouth declared, but am I any closer to the angels than they are…good angels or bad angels, perhaps not a fake, but a freak?

Avoiding such questions, I get my pilgrims to tell me about *their* good and bad angels. The trick of loving one's neighbour as one's self is, partly at least, the knack of finding *his (*or *her)* story as fascinating as one's own; (- who said it would always be easy?!). As I observe each struggle to adapt the familiar autobiography to suit the novel circumstance of telling it to a hermit 50ft up, the moment might come-a, for them, revelatory deviation from their "authorized" version. THAT moment alone may be worth their trip.

We're getting on -pilgrims, angels, lost souls, walls, belief and disbelief! Is even "truth" in there some where, at least by implication? - Perhaps that's the best we can ever hope for: how many balls have we in the air already? Fifty years ago I knew a juggler who could manage ten at once, and I reassured an emperor - *the* Emperor, recently (who puts great faith in **walls** incidentally,) - helping to settle a controversy, reassured him that Christ when he was here among us was *two* things at once; divine *and* human. Official dogma now; they've built a wall round it, and for every truth, it follows that there are the attendant heresies and all that they entail.....All the cruelty in the world is inflicted by those who believe they are in the right:*(gravely but lightly, with a gesture as if floating a small air ball towards his audience)* - discuss.

There was a moment during my correspondence with the Emperor when it seemed that he might visit me. This marble chair

Pillar Talk ══ 13

was sent ahead; quite a business hauling it up. He didn't visit me, but wrote that it might still come in useful if ever I needed to try out what it felt like to be Pope. I haven't availed myself. Empathy aside, measuring one's estate by that of others, though it is the engine of healthy competition, invariably leads to pride or envy. It is not my will alone, nor entirely God's that holds me up here; I seem to have chosen but there is a great web spun of the voluntary and involuntary actions of...... millions. That is the infra-extra structure on which I really stand. I daresay the Pope on his throne knows as much, even as he exercises his power to keep certain cardinals standing in his presence.

As for my pillar - from your perspective you will have already associated my position with a certain crude symbolism perhaps, or with stunts, ivory towers. ...I've a lot of time for the sword of Damocles, (talking of stunts) - I've a lot of *time*... I hope it won't seem too much for you. Intimations of eternity are all very well - up to a point...Damocles of Syracuse the courtier - the story is some seven hundred years old from where I'm standing but perhaps worth skipping through;-lighten and quicken the tone - artificial move left to keep it alive - Damocles had been extolling what he believed to be the perfect royal happiness of the Tyrant of Syracuse, Dionysus. Now Dionysus- no relation to the God, though he liked his wine - being a Tyrant, was told of what Damocles had been saying.

"My perfect Royal happiness? he said, *that's the first I've heard of it! This calls for a celebration!"* ...- and Damocles found himself mounting the familiar cool marble staircases, the air especially sweet, he noticed, with the perfume of flowers. Soon he was bandying small talk amongst the great, (which so often gives the impression of being superior to great talk amongst the small). His delicious sense of being at the centre of the universe… - I suppose that Damocles thought that Dionysus carried the centre of the universe, or at least Syracuse, round with him in his pocket… - at any rate, Damocles knew he was *where it was at*, and the sensation was pleasantly intensified when, at the banquet, he was assigned a place next to Dionysus in the most charmed of all charmed circles. He had hardly noticed amongst the splendid decorations - there were so many - the gleaming unsheathed sword suspended, as in thin air, by a single hair taken from the tail of a white horse.

No one ever mentions the horse, but there it was at some stage, standing all unsuspecting without a thought in its head. *(Pause)* It is decades since I saw a horse's head close up- a great noble sight…

…those soft eyes - *(runs his hand down the imagined length of the horse's head from fore head to nostrils)* - and not a thought behind them that we would call a thought. No *mind*. Interesting how some rival religions set great store by emptying the mind. The white horse - all unsuspecting… *(mimes plucking the single hair and the horse's reaction)*

Something in Damocles' mind, sixth sense, horse sense? - made him look up to find that he had been placed directly beneath that sword.

I had a famous Roman actor come up to me not so long ago, who'd always felt, he told me, that his success had been hanging by a hair. "Fame" he said "is the only thing worth having for an actor". He sat there to begin with, *(indicating the stool)* and was rather out of breath I remember and said, "I rode up your hill in search of a sign; the first I saw read, "No camels or horses beyond this point!"

I stood..

As his fame had grown - the actor's - he'd got the choice of all the best parts, and his success in the best parts led to more fame, "It is a fragile cycle", he said, " to sustain it has demanded as much horse work and tenacity and luck as I always knew it would. I'm next to unassailable now, constantly referred to as "great" and the time is coming no doubt when I shall be part of the theatre's glorious past whilst I'm still present, but now, on the crest of what seems to be a perpetual wave, I have begun to feel an undertow of grief...my choice of words may be derivative, I'm an actor, and used to using other people's words, but I can assure you that the state I am trying to describe is primal. A nameless grief, I find myself, when alone, suddenly weeping" He wept as he told me this.

And is fame so very important I said. He turned on me;

"Tell me, what is the good, or even the possibility of a great sage or saint of whom nobody has heard? I never stumbled across you in your obscure desert cave when we were both young, even though it was not so very obscure", he said, " though I remember the night I heard that there was a strange young shepherd - turned monk - turned hermit called

Symeon, troubled by too many supplications for healings and blessings and absolutions and advice, who had left his cave - I still remember the lamplight as we actors listened and dressed before the performance, and how we laughed to hear that you had "escaped" to live on top of an eight foot stone pillar. - "Quick" I said, "Get me the name of his publicist".....he said.

"Your picture is sold in the streets of Rome! Like mine; you've come up in the world - higher estimation - higher pillar".

I wish you could all have heard him talk, he was continually   fascinating-

"Of course I'm fascinating," he shouted at me - "It's my job, and if you'd had to breathe life into the occasional cocked up classical adaptation and as much decadent second class Byzantine crap as I have, *you'd* be fascinating - or dead!!"

You can see why The Church felt she had to excommunicate the actors.

Then he wept for a while. "As it is", he said, "you are dead to the world and that's your fascination."

It's time I took a little exercise - (*solemnly stands, places his hands together, arms stretched high, then brings them down to crutch* *level, fingers interlocked, palms downwards. Suddenly he breaks into a short burst of activity reminiscent of an eccentric vaudeville dance; that's because it **is** an eccentric vaudeville dance; stops, leans on the non-existent wall to his right - very nearly falls off the pillar, starts to cross himself, but aware that there might be people below watching, turns the gesture into one of blessing the crowd .He sits)* That's all I needed.

After a while, I ventured to say to our actor - "You will, perhaps be familiar with the story", - and so may you - of the distinguished physician of Antioch who received a new patient one day. The man sat simply and gravely in front of the physician and said "Do you have a cure for unhappiness?"

"Let me examine you first" the doctor responded, and found him to be unusually strong and healthy. He was a good doctor and said, "I may have just the thing. I have a token for the circus; laughter is a great restorative - you must take this", and he put the token on the table, "Go and see Aleppio the wonderful clown." The man looked at the token and did not move and after a moment said simply,

"I go there every day - I **am** Aleppio" "

"Yes" our great actor said, I am familiar

with the story. Too familiar; it is apocryphal of course; the flux of existence rarely forms itself into elegant patterns of satisfyingly significant irony and paradox: if it did we'd have no use for story tellers and priests, relics and souvenirs or even circuses.

Like you", he said, "I am a purveyor of form and of stories, and though I nod and sometimes bow low in the direction of the primacy of text, I'm in the front line as a ***celebrant***. We actors turn even the brackish backwaters of human intercourse into palatable wine. Centuries ago, the comedian Roscius, born a slave, instructed Cicero in elocution, and we still remember his name, though what his *magic* was we can never know!" - and he babbled about some stage business he'd seen when he'd been a young man. A famous actor of the time in a long outmoded and forgotten play lived on in his memory simply because of the way he had entered and stood and said... what was it "Good Day" I think-" am I late?"

He explained,

"It was not a history in a look, an epoch in a gesture, nor a seismic shift in the turn of a head (I've seen that done) - it was much smaller than that. It was a tiny moment in the story of a Mr. Nobody Everybody, so truthfully recorded...

we smiled…We… I admit, I've mythologized it, put it up on a pedestal."

(*pause*)

He asked about this chair and said, "I don't need to sit on an authentic throne to imagine being Pope; I can imagine being any body, anybody! It's the unimaginable inconvenience of being me that's the trouble" He touched the chair - "Good prop though," and he sat in it and gave an imperial wave to the little crowd that had gathered below. "Nice bit of publicity" he said.

He told me he had a son somewhere and had had many loves but none he had loved more, or even as much as himself. – "To compound it all my acting has lent a romantic dignity to the sword – even though I have only ever used a wooden one: the sword, that instrument of butchery which your faith has so signally failed to discredit as the instrument of justice and peace. How then can you rescue me from the war in my heart and mind? Surgery?

"On my pedestal of fame, I am like you on your damned holy pillar, nurturing nothing and no one but the magnificent spectacle of your faith and religion, exemplifying nothing but yourself"

(*pause*)

Faith is not to be sniffed at, as all of you who have ever lit a candle and muttered a prayer know.

I must tell you all something I told him...

Just occasionally of late, I have been aware of...how can I describe it... of a delicate membrane, quite close, an invisible veil, just to my right for some reason. Perhaps the sky is particularly beautiful, or it is night and underneath the stars my local nightingale is singing and quite suddenly, the membrane is there. On the other side of it is despair. What has prevented me stumbling through it all these years...?

"The cure," my actor responded," if you ever join me on this side of the veil would be to go and test the remnants of your faith and work as one the poorest and cruellest used vassals - there are plenty of them - where you would at least have the yearning and hope for freedom to sustain you, and could marvel at the songs that are sung in chains; perhaps join in. Come down, come down; engage, risk, care, act - at the very least milk the goats, bottle the olive oil. Drop the Latin and fine talk become a shepherd again. But no," he said as he began to go down the ladder, "we are both really too secure in our successful routines to risk change, and I must rest before tonight's performance. On the stage I know where I am and on a good night I may give, or even get, a fleeting impression that all this is, as we say in the theatre, - ***worth the candle…***"

(pause)

I gave him my blessing as he descended…

…then, on an impulse called to him,

"Find a scene in which you are not the monarch or the warrior with his sword, but the white horse,"

He stopped dead on the ladder, and after a moment shouted down to his troupe of companions "Props! Knock up a horse's mask for tonight in time for act four, a white one"

(pause).

The day goes on down there. My disciples are milking the goats amongst the olive trees. "Fresh Goats cheese from the farm of The Brethren of Simeon Stylites; good enough to give up for lent." They've opened the little stall where you can buy my prayers and prophesies… There's the dog that barks and wags his tail at me. He's busy relieving himself. I can see the patient vulnerable look in his eyes from here. *(Pause)* That's better. (We *hear the dog bark twice; Simeon barks back in echo)* Now he's scampering off on the hunt…. and there ***we*** are, somewhere between him and the angels. You must have been wondering about my … arrangements. There is a basket and bucket pulley system. Food, gifts letters and my replies come up and go down in the basket. Needless to say the bucket ...(a small bell rings,) Timing! (perhaps Symeon himself turns a handle to draw something up.) It takes a while…Don't worry; this is going to be the basket. I mentioned the juggler - there's just time, I told our great actor about him. It must be fifty odd years ago, when I was a novitiate monk, he was discovered asleep under our portico. He was perhaps fourteen, had been abandoned by a travelling circus. His poor parents had sold him into the circus when he was quite small. I daresay they thought he wasn't "all there", his mouth wasn't properly formed. The Abbot got his story out of him. They had taught him to clown and juggle, and he'd learnt the life and death trust and discipline of the trapeze. (*Simeon mimes two hands reaching and catching as in a trapeze act)....*in which the phrase "give me your hand" really means something.

"But why did they leave you behind?" our abbot asked?

It seems that one day they had captured a young lion and the boy learnt for the first time what cruelty was used to deprive such a creature of its liberty, tame it and teach it to do tricks, and he took to sitting by its cage or with the elephant and weeping and the circus people didn't trust him on the trapeze anymore.

The Abbot had been rather shocked, for the lad had said of wild animals, "There are things they know that we don't". But he was given a place to sleep in the barn and did menial tasks. He was good with the farm animals and he would creep into a dark corner of the chapel and kneel listening to us singing, and sometimes I would glimpse him as we processed out at the end of our service. One hot day we had been gathering a splendid harvest in our orchard and we had decorated the altar and the window ledges with fruit to give thanks and ask for blessing. It so happened in the middle of that hot night that I woke and went to the chapel to pray, and there in front of the alter in the moonlight was the boy. I think I counted ten peaches in the air as he juggled and cavorted. It was like a miracle, but it was not an illusion, nor a trick. It was real. I had only ever seen the little bands of tumblers who used to come through our poor village when I was a boy, never an acrobat as light and skilled and graceful as our young drudge. He looked like an angel (*Pause, The*

Pillar Talk 25

winch stops. Pause; Simeon lifts a little panel out of his platform floor and unhooks a lidded basket from the mechanism, and sets it aside having taken out of it a bottle of water. He presses the bottle to his forehead for a moment then he drinks.)

Who needs miracles - life is the miracle. The taste of this water! It explains the miracle at the wedding feast at Cana.....

Shortly afterwards the order ejected me because of my excessive austerities - there's a contradiction in terms - (the abbot said that I should give up my austerities for lent) and I took to my cave. And up here, to cut a long story short, I am.

(Pause)

Another sunset… (*He rises and takes a turn about the platform. The dog barks from far below. Simeon stops, looks down to the right, gently waves, and leaning on the forth wall, barks back in a whisper, then he goes and sits and opens the box. Night falls. The stars come out. Symeon, opening the lid of the basket is surprised to find what else it contains, gently closes the lid and puts it to one side.*

Moonlight floods the platform.

Simeon's hands come together in the conventional prayer position. He opens his eyes and looks at them.) There's another miracle, *(observing his fingers interlocking and unlocking.)* only visible when the thick veil of habit and routine blows aside. *(Pause)* What should I give thanks for tonight? What are the transgressions I should confess? - Not the old war horses of vanity, pride - or carnal lust, (chance would be a fine thing) - but the realization that my habit of talking to you *(looking up)* is just that, a habit - a routine…..

Who are you? What is this - "I". *(Pause)*

I haven't forgotten my difficult question: I'm going to change the symbolism of your position; I'm going to imagine that you are there.

(Looks off left into the wings, and from now on he occasionally looks towards the wing, as a comedian might look, defiantly? apprehensively ? - towards that mythical stage manager.) My question. It's rhetorical.

And God so loved the world that he sent a child into it - uniquely precious like all God's children - a boy, or a girl, whose father was perhaps a carpenter; and the child grew and learnt, and its mother watched as the sun shone into the little house and beamed along the shelf of wooden toys her husband had made, and gilded the child's first crude creative efforts, and sweetly she sang the songs her mother had sung to her. And it came to pass that a great wave swept away the house and the family and a thousand other families and broke every last domestic detail of their lives. And in its wake there were many acts of courage and strength and kindness as well as violence and selfishness, but of the child's family and many, many others, there was no trace, nor anyone left who had known them, so that no story was ever told about them, nor any name remembered.

Before I woke the other day, I was hovering above my pillar like a sky lark and I couldn't wait to wake up to demonstrate my new found blessed ability to the world. The instant I did wake up, I felt the wingless weight of my body on the stone, and before I even opened my eyes I knew, with all the terrible weight of incontrovertible experienced truth, that it was sky larks who flew. I could hear his song. I looked up at the sky to see him, - an ordinary sky lark locked in his miraculous daily routine as I am in mine, neither of us knowing why, and he too ecstatic to ask. Dreams. Do skylarks dream? Dogs do.

Dramatic entrances with doves descending from heaven...Our Dreams; and as for the other ascensions and descensions……..they tell me less than the skylark knows.

(He is still for a while with his eyes closed, then he feels towards the basket and, eyes still closed, takes out three peaches, holds them close with his head bowed. The nightingale begins to sing. He opens his eyes and hesitatingly begins to attempt to juggle with the fruit. He stops after a moment and looks at the audience.)

This business will need a lot more rehearsal before it's worth watching - go in peace...

(He resumes his attempt at juggling. The nightingale sings on. Very soon, Symeon places the three peaches on the marble chair. It is the first time it has been touched. He pulls up his hood and lies down on the floor of the top of his pillar to sleep. Darkness falls.)

The End

AFTERWORD

What went into the moulding I made of a fanciful terracotta Symeon on the top of his pillar? A rudimentary technique - which I half hoped, as I worked, was giving it the air of something to be found at the back of a glass case of minor Byzantine finds at the British museum, though I knew in my heart that in the company of such objects, it would cry out that it came from the Camden Arts Centre pottery class for the culturally bewildered in the Finchley Road one Wednesday morning in the early Spring of 2005. The skilled, imaginative young artist in ceramics who teaches us there, and whose mission on Wednesdays must be to find sermons in stones and good in everything, was charmingly encouraging to this white haired eccentric, the only man in her group - and who am I to doubt her sincerity? - but whether one is working (or playing) in words or clay, (or charcoal on paper on Thursday afternoons) - whatever one's technical accomplishments or limitations, things have a tendency to come out as *they* want to - they force or insinuate their way through one's clevernesses and incompitences. Indeed one way of looking at technique - I don't know whether the word is used or even permitted in artistic circles any more - and whether the lion's share still goes to perspiration rather than inspiration - still, one way of looking at technique is to practice and practice and practice until one has the knack and the confidence gracefully to stand aside and give the 'art' a chance.

The painter Braque thought of it another way, and certainly thought of cubism – "his" cubism - as "a means to bring painting within reach of my own talents."

In this acting script, I've tried to bring something of the life of an impossibly remote religious figure within reach of my own acting talents. (You will sympathise with my simple faith, that after fifty years on the stage I would be on terra firma there.) I may tell you that the man who teaches "critical life drawing" on Thursday afternoons in the Camden Arts Centre, exhorted us one day to look at the model for two minutes, then close our eyes and draw with both hands, " as if "he said " you are modelling clay."

That day I went out into the traffic ridden Finchley Road, very near where a woman in white put her hand on Walter Hartright's shoulder and asked "Is this the road to London" – (Wilkie Collins, as you may know, married an actual woman in white whom he had seen immerge into the road from Hampstead in the moonlight one night.) - It occurred to me that evening in the wings of the Palace Theatre as I heard the familiar strains of the orchestra playing, for perhaps the hundred and fiftieth time, Andrew Lloyd Webber's music introducing my entrance as Wilkie Collins's Mr. Fairlie - it occurred to me that it would be nice if I could close my eyes and, using both hands, realise Mr Fairlie sculpturally, metaphorically speaking, in wet terracotta for a change.

So keen were they in Antioch to have the body of Symeon as a holy relic after he died that they sent 600 soldiers to make sure they got him. During his life we are told that pilgrims made journeys to see him from as far away as Britain. One supposes that he spent his life confronting the problem of Good and Evil, as we do in our way. One morning, a few days after I'd completed writing the first draft my little play, something happened in a street of wealthy houses off the aforementioned Finchley Rd., round the corner from the Central School of Speech and Drama, a well dressed man carrying an axe, coolly, according to eyewitnesses, approached another, older man, and actually did, only too thoroughly, what many of us in extremis have only imagined doing, apparently, allegedly, in this case according to press accounts, to settle an old score.

If a pilgrim who journeyed from the west sixteen centuries ago to witness the glories of the Christian Eastern Empire, somehow were to slip into today's Finchley Road, he would find the scene bizarre in the extreme and, leaving axes aside, find sin alive and beyond the nightmares of Byzantium. Perhaps he would wonder why none of us had taken to living on pillars.

******

ABOUT THE AUTHOR

Edward Petherbridge's *Pillar Talk* celebrates his fiftieth year as an actor and provides him the part of St. Symeon Stylites, performed at the Pleasance in the Fringe Festival 2005; accompanied here by two witty essays charting journeys to Syria and Bradford in search of inspiration. Memorable roles to-date are Guildenstern in Stoppard's *Rosencrantz and Guildenstern are Dead,* NT '67-'7O, his Newman Noggs in the RSC's *Nicholas Nickleby,* London and Broadway, 1980-82 (available now on DVD) - Lord Peter Wimsey in BBC TV's Dorothy L. Mayors Mysteries (also available on *DVD).* He played Malvolio and Master Ford for the RSC in the late '90s, as well as Samuel Beckett's "Krapp". C. D. s of his poetry and prose are collectors' pieces. He is an Hon.D.Litt of Bradford University.
www.pethsstagingpost.com

Lightning Source UK Ltd.
Milton Keynes UK
UKHW011708260421
382648UK00003B/912